· T H E ·

PRINCESS
DIARIES · 2

ROYAL ENGAGEMENT

Movie Scrapbook

Based on characters created by Meg Cabot
Screenplay written by Shonda Rhimes

SCHOLASTIC INC.

New York Toronto London Auckland Sydney
Mexico City New Delhi Hong Kong Buenos Aires

ISBN 0-439-68478-1

Cover designed by Louise Bova

Interior designed by Maria Stasavage

12 11 10 9 8 7 6 5 4 3 2 1   4 5 6 7 8 9/0
Printed in the U.S.A.
First printing, September 2004

Once upon a time, a princess kept a diary, in which she recorded all her hopes and dreams. That would be me, Mia Thermopolis, once an ordinary high school girl, now, princess of the principality of Genovia. This entry is about Prince Charming.

More specifically—about not having one!

The more I get to know the Genovian people, the more I love them, especially my Grandmother, Queen Clarisse Rinaldi. That's her in the front [left] of this snapshot. See that follically-challenged guy to Grandmother's right? That would be Joseph, her footman and just maybe *her* prince charming . . .

There's a saying, "Uneasy lies the head that wears the crown."

I say: *not*! Wearing the crown of a country you're dedicated to feels just right. Which is a good thing, since I'm soon to become queen.

Speaking of feeling just right? When I danced with this guy, I didn't even know his name. I found out it was Nicholas—just before I klutzily stepped on his foot. I hope I don't become known as Queen Klutz of Genovia!

This is the day I explored the palace.

This is the day I accidentally came upon a secret tunnel.

This is the day I overheard something I wasn't supposed to . . .

. . . and wigged out! Not because the members of Parliament wear old-fashioned shoulder-length white wigs, but because of another old-fashioned custom they were talking about: the one that says if there's a *guy* heir to the throne, *I* have to be married to ascend to queen! What century are we in??

Whatever. This is a total non-issue. There *is* no male heir to the throne of Genovia.

Or is there? Remember cutie-pie dance partner? The one whose foot I stepped on? Wish I'd stepped down harder. Nicholas Devereaux—Nick Devious to me [that's his uncle, Viscount Mabrey]—is challenging me!

I look surprised in this photo. I am surprised. And *so* not in a good way.

It's not that I have this need to rule. In life, you play the hand that's dealt you. Becoming Queen of Genovia is my duty, it's what my grandmother has been training me for. It's my dad's legacy. No one can take that away from me.

Even if I do have to . . . gulp . . . get married.

It gets worse. I have thirty days to find Prince Charming, snare the ring, and make it to the altar.

And worst. Nicholas, "Prince *Not* Charming," gets to live at the palace. Which is where *I* live.

He is not cute. He is not gorgeous. He is not hot. Maybe if I keep repeating that, I'll believe it. Or—I just won't look at him.

My bedroom is posh, princess-pretty, pillow-packed, and totally private. Being there almost makes me forget about you-know-who and that whole you-know-what thing. Almost.

Meet the requirementally-suitable Andrew Jacoby, Duke of Kenilworth. So would that make me Mia Jacoby or Mia Kenilworth? Or Mia Culpa?

"Getting To Know You" is a song from the musical *The King and I*. It's what Andrew and I are doing in this less-than-private beach stroll.

With the very nice and presentable Andrew on my arm, I get to announce my engagement, and thereby secure my rightful place as Queen of Genovia. Take *that*, Nicholas, pretender boy!

Notice any family resemblance 'twixt Nick and Mabrey? I don't either.

So that's that. Andrew's in, Nick's out. I will be queen, Nick will be . . . out. But he keeps showing up. With that face, those eyes . . . no! I will just *not*. And that's that. Or did I already say that?

When you're really in love, you can hear music even when there is none. And dance to it. Or so I've been told. Memo to self: try with Andrew.

One day, I hope to be as cool as my grandmother. She's absolutely regal. Beautiful, graceful, smart, Queen Clarisse always knows the right things to do and say.

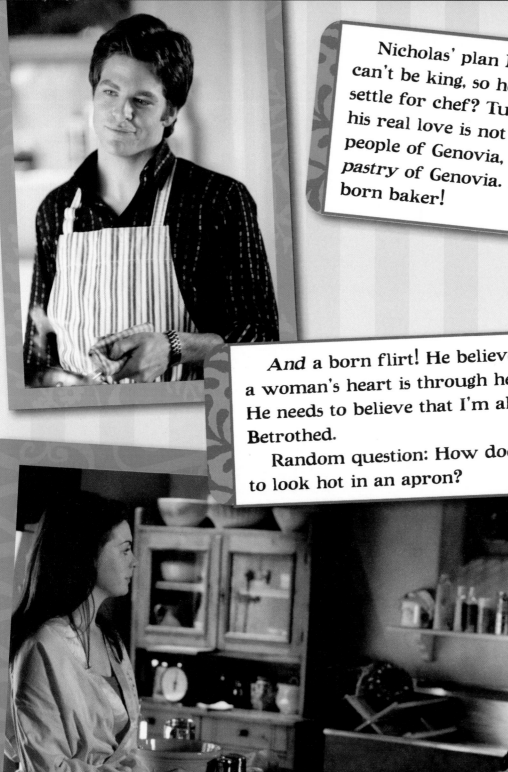

Nicholas' plan B? He can't be king, so he'll settle for chef? Turns out his real love is not the people of Genovia, but the pastry of Genovia. He's a born baker!

And a born flirt! He believes the way to a woman's heart is through her taste buds. He needs to believe that I'm already taken. Betrothed.

Random question: How does he manage to look hot in an apron?

Tricks of the trade: the royal edition. A wooden leg, when attached properly, can fool folks into assuming you're riding sidesaddle. That's the Gran-plan.

How's this for prim and proper pony posture?

Tricks of the trade: schemer edition. A kid was bribed to scare my steed, which reared up and scared the onlookers, which scared Joseph . . . who tried to save me. Accidentally pulling off the wooden leg in the process. Which scared me. *Big* time.

Remember I said Grandmother always knows just what to do? It may not look like it from this friends-with-the-enemy photo, but I have faith in Queen Clarisse.

Nicholas has a date. Her name is Alyssa. They make a lovely couple. Not. She's awfully dreary if you ask me.

Uh-oh! Is the queen of uncoordinated at it again? A one-up spar with Nicholas resulted in an unplanned dunk in the pool. Which wasn't completely horrible.

Grandmother and I, with the ever-watchful Joseph, attend the Genovian Independence Day parade via royal carriage.

My heart so goes out to the littlest Genovians. These are orphans, but I will make them feel special today.

This is what it's all about. Putting smiles on these faces is what makes me feel like a real princess-about-to-be-queen. This is when I know I am doing the right thing, even if it means making sacrifices.

Viscount Mabrey is determined. He will not give up trying to push me aside so Nicholas can be king.

Trying to get my attention, Nicholas throws pebbles at my window. Sweet, only he's at the wrong window.

Following Lilly's advice combined with my own klutziness-strikes-again is what landed me in this very un-princess-like position!

Following my own heart—a little—led me to the lake with Nicholas.

Unbeknownst to us, a camera-toting spy was ordered to follow us. He wasn't alone. The Genovian paparazzi had us staked out.

I give up. He *is* dreamy. And nice, and smart and funny and he makes me feel beautiful and adored. Could he be my Prince Charming?

Or has Nicholas betrayed me? I don't know what to think.

No pretending to ride sidesaddle now. My need is for speed. Grandmother and Lilly probably think I've disappeared.

Score one for the paparazzi. Videos of Nicholas and me are all over the news. And have I mentioned today's my wedding day?

Nicholas finds out the truth from his uncle's maid. Viscount Mabrey tipped off the press.

On a mission to stop the wedding, Nicholas hops atop the only set of wheels he can find.

A tender moment between Grandmother and Joseph.

Here comes the bride! I look amazing.
So why does it feel all wrong?

As usual, it's Grandmother with the right answer. In her heart she knows I should become queen. But she also knows that my heart is not in this wedding. She advises me to listen to it.

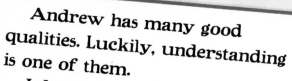

Andrew has many good qualities. Luckily, understanding is one of them.

I decided to channel my inner Grandmother and declare that even without a husband, I should, and would be queen!

Preparations for a royal wedding would not go to waste. Joseph convinced Grandmother to follow her own heart, and marry him.

I am free, single, and about to be queen. I am totally psyched!

In my robe, I test-drive the throne.

On one knee, Nicholas proposes—no, not that. Marriage isn't something you rush into. But love, that's something you fall into.

We did. That's when our music started.

PRINCESS DIARIES·2

Princess Mia . . . . Anne Hathaway

Queen Clarisse . . . . Julie Andrews

Nicholas . . . . Chris Pine

Andrew . . . . Callum Blue

Joseph . . . . Hector Elizondo

Lilly . . . . Heather Matarazzo

Viscount Mabrey . . . . John Rhys-Davies

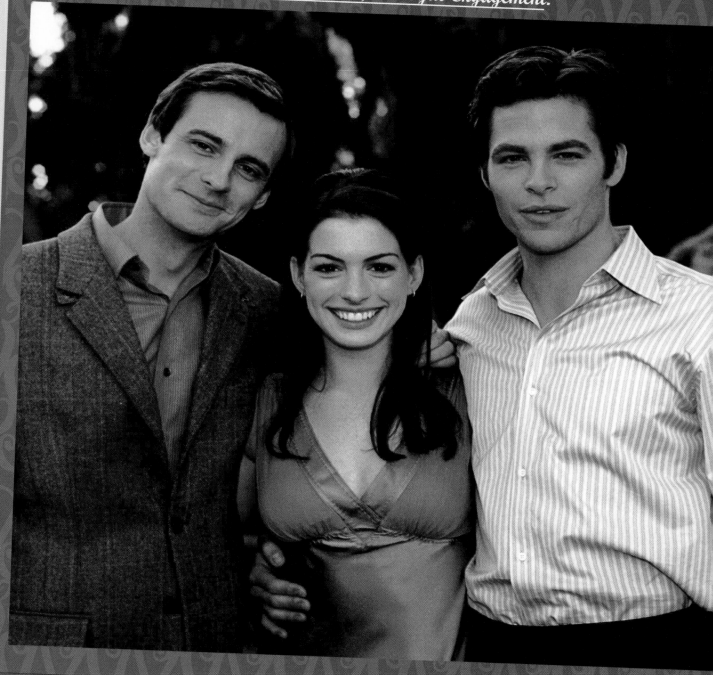

Callum Blue, Anne Hathaway, and Chris Pine are the stars of Princess Diaries 2, A Royal Engagement.

Anne Hathaway
"Princess Mia"

This is not the first time Anne has worn a tiara. She has also appeared in *Princess Diaries* and *Ella Enchanted*. Anne grew up a tomboy in New Jersey. Today, this twenty-one-year-old vegetarian is a student at Vassar College, where she's majoring in English. When she's not hitting the books, Anne enjoys listening to jazz, cooking, and sleeping in late.

Garry Marshall and Anne Hathaway

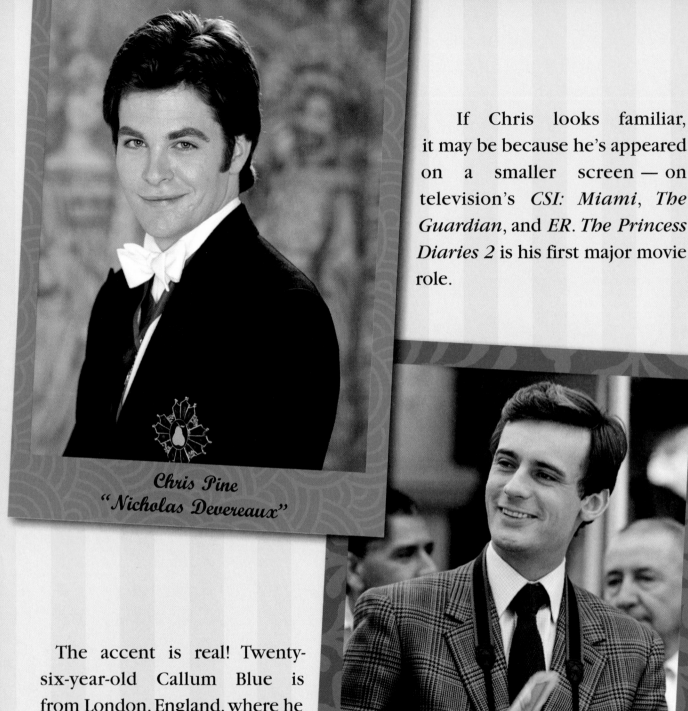

If Chris looks familiar, it may be because he's appeared on a smaller screen — on television's *CSI: Miami*, *The Guardian*, and *ER*. *The Princess Diaries 2* is his first major movie role.

Chris Pine
"Nicholas Devereaux"

The accent is real! Twenty-six-year-old Callum Blue is from London, England, where he studied acting at the Mountview Theater School. *The Princess Diaries 2* isn't his first acting gig. Callum has also appeared on television and in the feature film *Young Blades*.

Callum Blue
"Andrew Jacoby"

Julie Andrews has been on stage since she was four years old! She's appeared in many Broadway productions, and has also starred in many movies, like *Mary Poppins* and *The Sound of Music*. Julie also writes books for children, including *The Last of the Really Great Whangdoodles* and *Mandy*. She lives in England.

Julie Andrews
"Queen Clarisse"

Hector Elizondo had wanted to be a history teacher, but then the acting bug bit him! Since 1970, he's been in over eighty movies, including *Pretty Woman* and *Runaway Bride*. In his free time, Hector enjoys kendo (a type of Japanese fencing) and playing the guitar.

Hector Elizondo
"Joseph"

Chris Pine, Anne Hathaway, and Callum Blue